Aftereffects

Jiye Lee

First published March 2021 by Fly on the Wall Press
Published in the UK by Fly on the Wall Press
56 High Lea Rd, New Mills, Derbyshire, SK22 3DP

www.flyonthewallpress.co.uk
Copyright Jiye Lee © 2021
ISBN: 9781913211516

Acknowledgments

My gratitude extends to my family and incredible friends who have helped me through some difficult times whilst writing these poems. Sue, Gill, Rue, Jenny, and Rose, thank you especially for the encouragement, laughter and advice along the way. I also owe many thanks to my Creative Writing professors at Newcastle University whose guidance and support have been invaluable to my learning process.

A huge thank you to Isabelle Kenyon for bringing these poems into the world; for her hard work, commitment, and passion in amplifying the voices of so many writers who need to be heard.

Lastly, I'd like to thank my father, Jung Yun Lee to whom this book is dedicated to. From you I learned resilience, strength, and love, and I would not be here today without you.

Contents

Enigma with a Blackbird

After Pablo Neruda, Enigma with a Flower

Grief. It has come silently. I did not know
it had perched, the black figure
that sits in my chest,
piecing itself a home,
twig by twig, scrap by scrap,
my heart: her barn, her rooftop, her part of the tree to claim —
how she settles there, uninvited.
She sheds feathers, 'til the blackness
of her body seeps into mine,
'til her talons curl around my throat.
She spreads her wings — for a moment,
I breathe. Leaves behind an empty nest;
I hear a crack.

The Aftereffects of an Earthquake

1. Ground Rupture
I start bleeding from my uterus
in the month of July
just when I thought the heat of summer
was dying out

2. Landslide
A tumour sits in my stomach,
grows heavier by the day.
It broils and broils
especially when Mother
slices my heart
each time
with her guillotine tongue.
Finally, it erupts, screaming
and screaming,
my organs swirl in the mud

3. Tsunami
Please ensure you have the following documents with you for
closure of account of 1. Original copy of grant of probate 2.Death
certificate of deceased 3. Passport of Executor / Administrator
4. Ensure that the Executor / Administrator is present in person
This may be more complicated than anticipated You, your sister
and mother may have to make another visit
Qatar AirAsia Flight tickets: 1800 RM, 600,000 Won seeing as
you are all beneficiaries D705 AirAsia Emirates

5. Your next counselling session will be 03/10
D.O.B 27/02/1961 Date of Death 19/07/2016 Sign here,
here, and here Lawyer charges: 6878 RM...

4. Liquefaction

I wake to the slippage
of dreams—
eyes still aflutter
    I'm alive,
       I'm alive,
you keep repeating
until I finally believe.
Tears ribboning down my face –
    I collapse.

The End of the Poem

On the days that he dozed,
my sister and I would creep on our bellies,
hands clawing into carpet moss,
eyes peeking over the edge
to see the big, lanky, dungeon man.

Scaling the wall, we tread silently,
holding in our giggles.
I take a strand of my hair,
put it up his nose,
tickling a keyhole.

Eyes open. We scream. He shouts.
Legs and arms scramble off the bed – *run!*
But the dungeon man is faster.
Locks us up, one in each crook.
I'VE GOT YOU NOW!
I squirm, kick, and squeal,
with all the strength a seven-year-old can muster.
I try to unscrew my bolted chest,
bars fastened tight. He smiles at my puny efforts
to wrestle free.
A further struggle: door gives way –
the perfect moment to slide out a hand,
wrench free a limb, leap from his chains.
Heart palpitating, scurrying feet,
a grin searing my face.
I catch my breath on the stairs,
ready to do it all over again.

The dungeon man
is   older now,   h as   l o st
his vo ice.

        He lies on the bed
eyes closed   as if he i s   sleeping
My heart   screams   WAKE UP!
The bars that used to hold me tight
          a bear's grip   safe   from the world
by his sides   stiff   unmoving

I take his hand
so terribly cold.

Last Breath

They say, when a person dies,
their soul is expelled from the body,
like a Heimlich burst.
Confronted with themselves on Earth,
they hover mid-air, grappling with the truth.

While Sister and Mother
see the body uncovered
at Al Haram Hospital in Cairo,
I grieve over the news
8480 km away in Seoul.

In another place,
does he wake to stirring sunlight,
the fading lustre of stars?
Hearing the murmurs of those who left
and came before him
riding the wind.

Would Father's first morning be like this?

Is his consciousness
suspended somewhere
circulating the universe?
Trying to find his way to heaven,
wandering;
with me, here on Earth,
wondering

How much does a minute weigh?

Rooms

In my Father's house there are many rooms. If it were not so, would I have told you that I go to prepare a place for you? And if I go prepare a place for you, I will come again and will take you to myself that where I am you may be also.

John 14:2-3

Entrance Hall
Recently, more than 470,000 Syrians
were put to death and displaced
trying to escape the civil war.
8000 dead and injured in Haiti.

Games Room
On a highway in Egypt, two vehicles collide.
Nobody cares to send help.
A father of two and his Egyptian driver
pronounced dead on the morning news:
no compensation.

Master Bedroom
God, does heaven have enough
rooms for all of this?
This chaos, these offences,
these innocent souls?

Attic
Do you have separate rooms for those
who face unjust, untimely ends?
Heaven must be heavy
with premature death.

Guest Bedroom
Is that why it rains?
The skies are unable to hold their tears?
Can Father really see us
from up there?

        Walk-in Closet
        They say heaven is a place that knows
        no more weeping,
        no more sadness, all misery washed away
        and sins atoned for.

Room 4
Does Father still smile
knowing how much it kills us
to live life with him gone?

Wolf and Buffalo

What can you do to save it now?
Come,
mourn it already.
My first meal of the day.
How else
will I survive motherhood?

December Ache

How does one empty the skies of thought?
How do I keep happiness
like a lifelong prayer?

I cannot bear the winters here.
Any scrap of sunlight,
the icy air snatches up whole.

Sometimes, I wonder what it would be like,
to be a snowflake
surrendering itself to the ground.

Is that what you'd call a beautiful death?

Assessment

There's a bridge. In Korea.
A well-known bridge,
I say

in response to her question,
Could you tell me in more detail as to how you thought of going about it?

Followed by the question,
Do you think about it now?

Sweet Mornings

There is a girl. There is a bed.
There is sunlight,
shining through sheer, white curtains.

There is the sound of a whirring fan
as she writes to the shrill cawing of birds,
their feet tapping on the condenser unit outside.

The girl has woken from sleep,
her first in four days.

To a baby, sleep is a given.
Mice, hedgehogs, and bears have the bliss of hibernating.
But to this girl, sleep is a dream fulfilled,
without meds, without nightmares.

Below, she hears Mrs. Kim shuffle.
The smell of freshly-baked bread,
the cardamom punch of Chai wafts up the stairs.

The Untouched

Dogs lounge on every pavement —
         black

                                    white

                    gold

                                      speckled

          sleeping

peacefully

        Cows   cross   the   road
                  the   driver
      waits   to   let   them   pass

On side streets
Goats amble

                              Camels sit untethered
                                 on dry grass

In the shopping centre, a stray dog bounces in
just looking around
McDonalds   *King's Waffles*   *E-bazaar*
until the security guards,
after having their laugh,
chase him out.

A Trip with My Ex-Boyfriend and His Parents

A lotus bud surrounded by minarets,
against a backdrop of ocean blue.
Clear waters, avenues of trees, flowerbeds —
It wasn't like this when I last came, he says.
This bit used to be filled with beggars.

Selfies by the reflecting pool. Climbing the steps
to enter the mausoleum, built by Emperor Shah Jahan
in memory of his wife, Mumtaz Mahal.
An old man jumps to my side. Shines his LED flashlight
back and forth on the inlaid stones of the marble screen.

Plain, gleams red
Rubee
Plain, gleams red
Rubee
I nod with open mouth, as if he is performing a magic trick.
   King
       Queen
I peer at the sarcophagi behind the screen.
The stone walls and marble floors breathe cold into my flesh.
Such a huge building. Such small bodies.

What's your name? he asks, eyes bright, moustache twitching.
Cocks his head back and shouts, *JEEEEEEEEEEE!*
Taking us in turns, he shouts each one into the air.
Do our names have a home now? Will this tomb keep them forever
safe? Encasing the dead and remnants of the living.

We go back outside, into the heat. Circle the plinth.
Study its symmetry, calligraphy inscribed on walls.
All this, for a woman, I exclaim.
No use when you're dead. Got to be good to her when you're alive,
my boyfriend's mother says, her husband two steps ahead.

Holding hands, we exit the mouth of the Taj Mahal.
Each step, sighing my reluctance to leave.
I imagine myself a princess, the glowing sunset my train.
From the pinnacles of red sandstone walls,
a monkey bids us goodbye with his butt.

I didn't enjoy it much the last time I came,
but seeing it with you felt different,
my boyfriend says.
I smile at him. See the minarets dissolve
and the sky weeping gold.

The Women in Goa

Your hair is so beautiful.
A nod.
Come,
I do braid for you darling.
A smile.
I give you good price.

Where did she learn that English accent?

How to put out a Forest Fire in June

1. Grab a helmet
2. Wear a mask
3. Don a firewoman's suit

Turn on the hoses from your eyes, your nose.
Every part of your body is a hydrant.
Ask God to make it rain – the same deluge he sent to Noah.

> In the centre of the forest
> rage the thickest flames –
> love,
> lust,
> longing,
> memories,
> happiness
> trust

neither flood nor tears can douse.

Three days ago, a fire in Maui burned 10,000 acres of land.
Thousands forced to evacuate, flights at Kahului airport diverted.

The longest a wildfire can burn
is up to fifty-two days.

The latest update: Firefighters continue to battle Maui wildfire,
reported 20 percent contained.

By the end of the first month,
I understand
the magnitude of this undertaking.

This fire took years for us to build.

After a Heatwave

I stop at the door, fumbling for my raincoat.
Raindrops are spitting down on slabs
gleaming charcoal black.
"Do you need an umbrella?"
the male receptionist offers,
the one that's always eager to help.

I step out, thankful for the generous cover
a *Primark* umbrella can afford
and walk into town with an 'I-actually-have-an-umbrella for once'
kind of confidence.
On Northumberland Street, a guy marches my way,
his umbrella reddish-brown

and broken.
Battling wind and water bullets —
its persistence like that of an autumn leaf.
I admire his indifference to the way he must look,
still holding it up above his head —
even lopsided protection is better than none.

Outside *Sports Direct* is the 'Opera guy' singing his set.
Hands in his pockets, taking shelter
underneath the awning.
In front of him, a woman,
grey-haired and thin,
is dancing barefoot in the rain.

The homeless man in front of Milligan's
sits upright,
his eyes seemingly bluer
against the backdrop of rain-washed streets;
wide and hopeful,
ready to meet the day.

The Other Country

flits through your mind like sunlight on a moving train.
You've heard what it's like from your parents.
Two summers ago, they took a cruise on the Red Sea,
breathed in the same salt air, crossed the shimmering waters
that Moses parted to let a nation pass and you wish
you could have seen it too.

You picture men in long, white dresses,
their sonorous voices, honey mouths,
belly laughter under a big, bright moon.
Arabic on jars, fruit on store shelves.
You imagine your father's first driver,
his face a brown umber. Eyes that speak.

Now, the other country has left a woman
widowed. How quickly the view changed
from a star-littered sky
to a car ablaze on the highway.
Poor Mother swallowed her screams,
journeyed back alone.

You wonder how it smells there.
Blink. You're greeted by a bleak sky, air clean and crisp.
Wet pavements, Royal Mail, and Yorkshire tea.
The other country falls
like a parachute in your mind,
crumpling softly to the ground.

In bed, you feel the sand blowing in your hair,
turbaned men leading you on camels.
Your father takes your hand
at the airport, at the door, welcomes you in.
Your mouth opens to speak
when a shadow flips over your eyes.

You discern five a.m. silhouettes of turrets and chimneys,
fumbling about in depths of murky blue
because you woke and couldn't fall back asleep,
the heat of the blazing sun still warm on your outstretched palms;
somewhere in the back of your memory,
Cairo's heartbeat thumps gently.

Samchon (삼촌 Uncle)

Leather jacket, sleek, black hair and sunnies,
strong scent of aftershave.
Mother said you were always popular with the girls.

You started your own business
selling bikes in summer, ski-equipment in winter.
Each year it grew

as did your beer belly.
Dyed your hair every three months in want of youth.
Changed your car from Hyundai, to BMW, to Land Rover.

Sylvia Plath killed herself through carbon monoxide poisoning.
Was she drunk, or sober? *Carbon monoxide —*
a colourless gas that has no smell or taste, initially non-irritating.

But you can't choke debt, Uncle.

When did it all go wrong?
Lending, investing, making deals over soju,
shaking hands you thought were clean.

What about Donghun, and So Yoon?
Wondering each day, why *Abba* won't come home.
Each night, they come crying in my dreams.

When they found your body in the car
inside the warehouse that kept all your stock — skis, snowboards,
winter coats, you were so badly decomposed.

How many days had it been since you did that?

Accident Anatomy

Upon leaving the house today,
I saw laid out between two white cars,
a body. One red fork protruding
from her plump belly, curled
as if grasping for air.
Her head was tucked
beneath her wing, stretched out
like a shield, moments before
the scream.
How peaceful she appeared
on the tarmac, stricken with sleep.
Her ashen feathers bleeding white
at the tips like angel wings.
I waited for her to stir.

Matheran Still Breathes on the Soles of My Shoes

                                        Six men push a wagon
                            loaded with slabs, boulders, and green pipes
                    up a winding hill—*huh, huh!*
            Calf muscles popping, veins ready to burst.
Their faces turn slowly,

eyes cold and silent
as I pass on my horse. Baba is silky black,
                    but his mane is as coarse as a shoe brush.
            Bridled, whipped, tugged, he plods along the rusty road.

Red letters corroded to brown: WELCOME TO MATHERAN.
            A hill station, a disused resort for the British.
            A colonial house weeps in a throng of twisted trees,
yellowing walls, windows curtained off and shut.
A soiled nameplate—*Spencer Villa*.
            I picture a long nose and dark moustache. Mr Spencer—
Tea trade tycoon? Head of the railway company?

A little boy in a green shirt sits in the folds of his mother's pink sari,
            her arms held above him, snapping away with a Nokia phone.
            At the hill station, a blue toy train is struggling for breath.
From the windows, their gazes pierce my back,
                            even as we ride away.

Back home, how gently the laterite falls

                   from the soles of my shoes.

        Reddish clay

dust

        still bearing the groans—*huh, huh!*—

the echoing clop, clop,

clopping

of hooves.

Signals

When my body sends me the signals,
> my eyes dwell on knives and their tips,

cracks in the fl o or b o a r ds of b r i d ges, the trees,

how they s w a y
> just before a tornado hits.

>> I think of the capsules in the bottle.

>> One s l i

>> p,

> and all the pain in my body

> f r e e d.

>> I look at cars whizzing by and think
>> of the impact

if I were to err just a little in my step.

> I looked up at the blue

and dreamed.

Now, only a shattered sky.

> *I thought about leaving this Earth,* Mother said
> after Father died.

But she didn't.

> I think of Uncle, who did.

I think about what Mother wanted to do,
> thought, how dare she contemplate such a thing.

> Thought, how could Uncle *do* such a thing.

But then, if I did what my uncle did,
> wouldn't that make me a fool, a hypocrite?

> This is the only thought that keeps me from doing it.

On days no more words come out of my mouth,
I look up to the sky,
recalling what my friend Chang Woo once said:

Even if the sky is falling,
there is still a teeny tiny   to escape through.

Arboretum Visits

That winter we went to visit you,
the ground was stripped of all its clothes.
It took us a while to find your tree.
Hi Charlie, Hi Dada — the two names
I loved to call you the most.
Merry Christmas.

That spring we went to see you,
the brook was trickling again but you
stayed covered in dead leaves.
For the first time, I did not shed any tears.
Was my heart so broken
all I could feel was an infinite zero?

That summer I went to see you alone,
everything was so much greener.
Each visit, my eyes need time to adjust.
I cleared away the dregs of winter
and laid a fresh bouquet of roses, canary yellow,
told you everything in my heart; my eyes a scalding ocean.

That autumn was the last I saw you,
Mother, Sister and me.
Mountain mosquitoes buzzing, delighted
to suck fresh blood. We walked back to the car,
cherries throbbing on our flesh.
Each time, so hard to leave.

Markings

On my forefinger is a tiny, chocolate freckle
that tells me I am my father's daughter.

Holding up his finger next to mine, he'd grin— *If someone ever tries*
to be your imposter, we'll know who our real daughter is.

Father took so much pride in that teeny tiny dot
but I couldn't wait to be rid of it—

hated the ownership it claimed, how it spoke of our bond
when in truth, there was so much distance between us.

I said I'd get it removed when I turned older,
didn't like the way it stood out, this random spot, conspicuous

molecule, like an ink mark that wouldn't go away.
Sometimes, I'd draw petals around it and turn it into a flower.

As time passed, the freckle began to lose its vitality—
from dark chocolate to pecan, it turned a lighter shade each year.

After God took Father away, you could barely see it
(like all that brown no longer needed my skin).

What I once saw as a genetic blemish, I see as a gift,
understand why he took so much pride in this tiny dot—

what that meant, to have your mark passed on,
ingrained in the flesh of someone you love.

Father, I do not need my hands
to know that I am your daughter.

Gifts

The sky was bright blue today,
the most beautiful I'd ever seen.

With a box-cutter,
I wanted to cut out a piece for you.

But then I remembered,
you already have this;
probably a much better view.

I wonder what the laughter of a tree sounds like.
If you ever laugh
when we come to visit you.

In between the 4th and 5th

I first titled this poem
Post-Grieving
but then realised,
Grief is an immortal word.

It has been exactly 1 year and 8 months.
Here, we are in that awkward month of transition —
my hands outstretched
ready to catch spring,
but winter's still tailgating from behind.

Carrying grocery bags on each side,
I am standing at the traffic lights.
The horizon before me,
boldly kissed by the sun,
now, a pure spot of gold sinking its way down,
turning buildings into shadows
whilst lipstick stains remain on each cheek of the sky,
still blushing.
Its flirtatious goodbye
leaves my heart
heavy
with longing.

I drop my bags, fumble for my phone.
As if, taking a picture would let this moment keep for longer,
let me keep something beautiful
so I don't miss it all the time.

I pray grief does not house itself here.

Tonight, I saw the moon
tattooed on April's skyline
with a Cheshire cat grin.
And for the first time,
I felt the seams of my own heart tear
into a smile
like the fluttering of a bird everybody thought dead.

And now I realise
I can write about beautiful things
not only because I imagine them
but because I have lost them.

Seollal (Korean New Year)

On the subway ride home,
I watch the little girl opposite me, passed out.
Her head pressed against the edge of the seat.

Her father worms out of his coat,
rolls it as best as he can, into a squished pupa.
Tipping his daughter's head to the side,
he plumps it into place against the partition;
lets her head fall back to a pillow of goose down.

The little girl
continues to dream.

About the Author

Jiye Lee is a British Korean poet from Newcastle. She focuses on themes of cultural identity, travels, family, mental health issues, love, and loss. She has been published in the journals *Literary Orphans, Bandit Fiction Press, Fragmented Voices*, and elsewhere. In 2019, her audio poem was commissioned by New Creatives North, a talent scheme funded by Arts Council England, Tyneside Cinema, and BBC Arts. Her work is forthcoming on BBC platforms. She is fascinated by true stories, the workings of different societies, people, and nature. Stories help her navigate this increasingly chaotic world, and poetry to process her own experiences and emotions.

Fly on the Wall Press

A publisher with a conscience.
Publishing high quality anthologies on pressing issues, chapbooks and poetry products, from exceptional poets around the globe. Founded in 2018 by founding editor, Isabelle Kenyon.
Social Media: @fly_press (Twitter) @flyonthewall_poetry (Instagram) @flyonthewallpress (Facebook)
www.flyonthewallpress.co.uk